Praise for

AUTOMATIC GOLF:

"I am amazed with the simplicity of the concept vs. its most gratifying results."

*"**Automatic Golf** added both length and accuracy to my game."*

"My score has been chopped by 10 strokes."

"More informative . . . than all of the books, articles and lessons I have taken for the past 30 years."

"The method is revolutionary and a great advancement for golf."

"I now enjoy playing golf again!"

AUTOMATIC GOLF

THE COMPLETE, ILLUSTRATED METHOD FOR LONGER, STRAIGHTER SHOTS

Bob Mann

♏ THE BODY PRESS

TUCSON, ARIZONA

Published by The Body Press, *A Division of HPBooks, Inc.*
P.O. Box 5367, Tucson, AZ 85703
Printed in U.S.A.   10 9 8 7 6 5 4 3 2
1st Printing

Book Design: Leslie Sinclair
Photographer: Larry Cole, Century City Photography
Golf Course: Valencia Country Club

Library of Congress Cataloging in Publication Data

Mann, Bob.
  Automatic golf.

  Includes index.
  1. Golf. I. Title
GV965.M235   1987   796.352'3   86-71871
ISBN 0-89586-508-4

DEDICATION

Automatic Golf is dedicated to the good news that an effective golf swing occurs as a natural response to proper muscle placement and movement. *Automatic Golf* is also dedicated to all of the good people who have helped me in developing this book.

CONTENTS

INTRODUCTION

Yours, mine and everybody else's golf swing falls into one of these three categories:

√ Beginner: Dominated by the wrists and arms, with very little body movement. Legs locked and upper body nearly immobile.

√ Average: Upper body active. Arms and wrists overactive. Legs nearly immobile.

√ Advanced: The more powerful muscles of legs and torso dominate. Upper body, arms and wrists merely respond.

This book shows you how to develop an advanced swing for longer, straighter shots, automatically.

When I turned professional in 1968, I began designing and manufacturing golf clubs. This led me to discover the reason most players can hit their short irons better than longer shots. Longer shots require far more dynamic action—action that can be produced only by using the large muscles of the legs and torso.

But it was not until after I had sold my business that I started to develop a teaching method that enabled golfers to use those proper swinging muscles.

THE SWING YOU DON'T HAVE TO THINK ABOUT

The result is *Automatic Golf.* The simple principles I've developed let a golfer achieve the right dynamic action needed to produce a successful and enjoyable swing. All of the mid-swing positions and features you have been striving for will occur properly as *effects,* caused by the pleasurable, dynamic action of the swing itself.

And so in 1982 I produced the *Automatic Golf* videotape. Its triple-platinum success proves that the method works. Already, more than 900,000 golfers have improved their game with it.

If you are new to the concepts in these pages, I assure you that longer, straighter shots will be yours very soon. All I ask is that you follow my instructions carefully and thoroughly. Since I made the video, I've had further "on-line" experience with golfers of all levels of ability and physical types. They've helped me hone the principles of *Automatic Golf* to an even simpler, easier-to-learn program. It's the step-by-step method you'll see here.

Whether you are new to the Automatic Golf method or not, I recommend that you practice these principles away from the golf course until your body tells you that you are ready to really give the ball the ride it deserves. It will happen sooner than you think!

Author's Note: The principles in this book will work for all golfers, whether you are right-handed or left-handed. Because I'm right-handed, the photos you see are for right-handed players. Lefties should simply read "left" for "right" and vice-versa.

ONE

THE AUTOMATIC GOLF METHOD

The Automatic Golf method does two very important things for your game:

1) It provides a "before-the-swing" procedure that allows you to create a *more dynamic motion* rather than a series of posed, structured or contrived swing parts.

2) It helps you identify, improve and strengthen a motion in which all of the things about your swing that have been troubling or eluding you simply clear up automatically, in the process of the swing itself.

But before getting into the mechanics of Automatic Golf, a parable is in order. I often use it to illustrate why the principles of Automatic Golf can work for me, you and everybody else who wants longer, straighter shots. I call it . . .

THE PARABLE OF THE JADE

A Chinese boy wanted to learn the jade business, and to this end arranged to learn under the tutelage of the local jade Master.

When the boy arrived for his first lesson, the Master handed him a piece of jade and told him to hold it tightly. As the boy sat holding the jade, the Master began to talk about everything under the sun . . . except jade.

This procedure (hold the jade, not talk about jade) was repeated for several days until finally the student's patience wore thin. He insisted that the jade lessons begin. The Master said, "Be more patient."

With the next visit, the Master handed the boy a stone that looked like jade but was not. As soon as the boy closed his hand he exclaimed, "That's not jade!"

There was wisdom in the master's method, and it applies to your golf swing too. Just as with the boy and the jade he held for days, you don't have to *know* the technical make-up of a good golf swing to experience it. You *know* when you produce a proper golf swing, and when you don't.

As you recall the "real jade," you'll acknowledge that you don't remember in which plane the swing occurred, how you cocked or uncocked your wrists or any of the other details that you have been asked to learn during your tenure as a golf student. You simply "know" a good golf swing when you feel it, just as the boy knew what real jade felt like.

The swing features that you have been striving for will happen automatically if your preparation and initial moves are correct. All of those mini-moves that you thought necessary to produce a good swing will simply occur as a product of the swing itself. You don't have to "do" them.

Another way of grasping this concept is to understand that a "grooved swing" is not the product of a practiced series of muscle-memorized mini-moves. A golf swing happens far too rapidly for you to assemble those mini-moves into one dynamic action.

You might say, "The swing, like life, is what happens while you're making other plans."

The very act of thinking through the golf swing destroys the dynamic action required to produce it. For example, wrist cock is an effect of the changing direction from backswing to downswing. Thinking about cocking the wrists, on the other hand, introduces a needless move that robs power and accuracy.

The list of effects that you have been trying to cause is quite long—wrist cock, plane, length of backswing, delayed hit, high finish, etc. On you go through a golfing career believing that if you learn this or that bit of minutiae, you'll create the magic swing.

If muscle-memorized mini-moves don't produce the "groove," what does? I'll show you. It's achievable. Moreover, it's easy.

CENTRIFUGAL FORCE

The groove is a product of centrifugal force. To visualize this, think about the slingshot that David used to slay Goliath. The mere whirling of the stone-weighted pocket created a grooved "swing" without any thought to details. What David *did* have to think about was:

1) Selecting the target.
2) Gripping the slingshot and loading the stone.
3) Starting the action.

The smooth grooved rotations were *responses* to this simple whirling move. Moreover, *David didn't do the swinging.* The loaded slingshot did that. The swinging was merely a *response* to the whirling David started.

MISCONCEPTIONS ABOUT CLUBHEAD SPEED

As you further visualize the action of David's slingshot, you will perhaps first reach an *incorrect conclusion* concerning the nature of clubhead speed. The tendency is to transform centrifugal force to golf by trying to generate clubhead speed with your hands, as David did. If this worked, we would whirl the club with our hand or hands as the hub of the action. There would be no backswing or downswing, just a whirl.

But the *correct* hub of the golf swing is the left shoulder, for a right-handed player. The slingshot is the *left arm along with the club*. The whirling motion is put into force first by the large muscles of the legs, torso and back—not by the hands.

What makes the golf ball go is the vibrating, dynamic energy stored in the shaft during the downswing and transferred through the clubhead at impact.

Many, perhaps most, golfers think that clubhead speed generated by the right hand "uncocking the wrists in a delayed hit" is what makes the ball go. In reality, this right-hand action does the reverse of what is intended—it reduces power by reducing the amount of energy stored in the shaft, energy properly gathered *only* through the application of centrifugal force.

A proper golf swing does not include any *conscious* cocking or uncocking action. The cocked position is achieved without thought or effort as the result of the swing's change of direction from back to forward (downswing).

The centrifugal force thus created causes the clubhead to properly lag. And this lag-delay is maintained through contact. Therefore, at contact, the hands lead the clubhead. Shaft energy compresses the ball, sending it on its way to the target. That marvelous sensation we experience when we hit it "solid" is thus achieved.

SIMPLIFYING THE SWING

When applied, the Automatic Golf method dramatically simplifies the swing, making it even simpler than the technical description you've just read. The product of that simplification is greater power (shaft energy) and greater accuracy (fewer moving parts). But even this knowledge, like the trivia I have asked you to "let go of," will not cause you to produce a better swing.

You simply can't "knowledge," or intellectualize, your way through a golf swing. If golf knowledge produced successful swings, long-driving contests would be won by those who read the most golf tips. You can't plan your way through a golf swing. The business executives aren't beating the pros.

But I've given you this technical analysis of what makes a golf ball go for two reasons:

1) To satisfy those who must intellectually understand a proc-

ess before they let go of it and do the simple things required to make it work.

2) To convince you to allow the swing to *occur naturally,* without trying to boost clubhead speed with the right hand.

The swing is not something that you "do." The swing is something that the club does *in response to a simple move that you make.* That's the essence of the rest of this book.

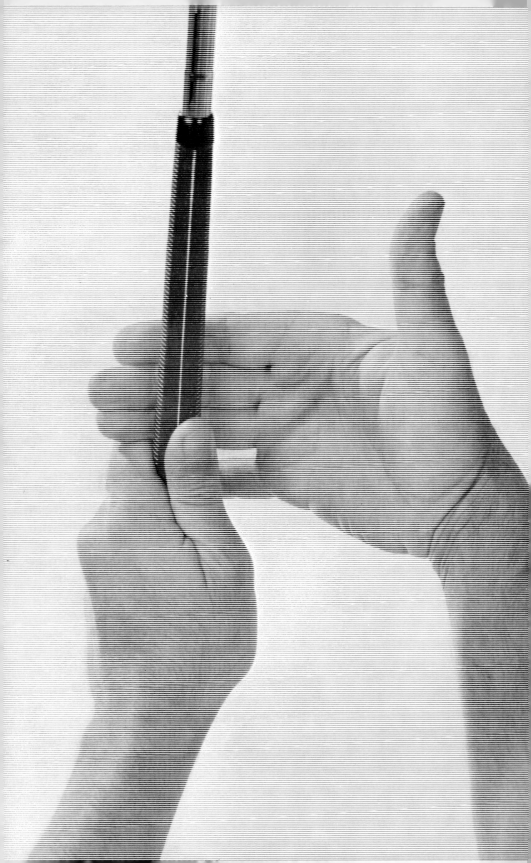

TWO
PRE-SWING PREPARATION

A good golf swing is simple and very pleasurable if un-complicated by your concern over plane, backswing length, de-layed hit, etc. But it's simple only if you *prepare it to be simple*. That's why I emphasize placing the right muscles in the right places.

THE AUTOMATIC GOLF GRIP

There is only one grip you can use to do all of the following:

√ Automatically create the proper relationship between your body and the ball.

√ From the start, place the proper swinging muscles in com-mand.

√ Create a club-arm relationship that allows the swing to occur without the clubface flopping, twisting or otherwise changing position during the swing. (This not only increases reliability by reducing moving parts, but also increases power by stopping the power leaks inherent to hand manipulations of the club during the swing.)

The basic functions of the grip are incredibly important in successful golf shots. That's why you must master the grip. Do it precisely and carefully, as described and pictured here.

You must place the hands on the club in a manner that supports the club and contains the dynamic action without inhibiting or actively "adding to." For this to happen most reliably, hold the club in the air, at approximately a 45° angle in front of you. (At this point, your right hand is merely holding the club up for the left hand to grasp. Final placement of the right-hand grip follows the left.)

Stand erect and raise your club *just below* the grip with the right hand. Hold the club at arm's-length in front of the (approximate) centerline of your body, right hand at chest level.

Club angle should be approximately as shown below—not as shown in either of the pictures opposite.

CORRECT

INCORRECT

INCORRECT

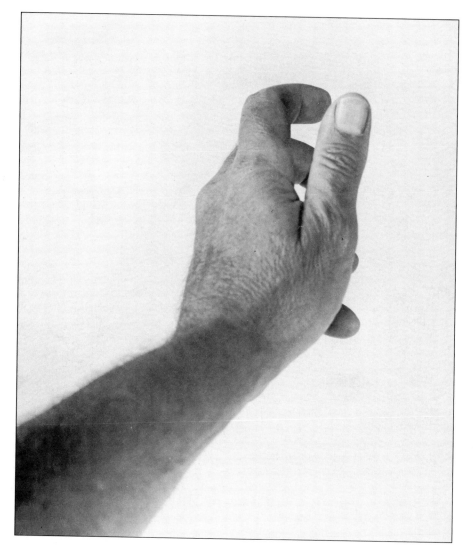

LEFT HAND

Rotate the left hand (for right-handed players; opposite for lefties) until the thumb is just to the right side of the centerline as you look down at your hand. You will see two knuckles: Top knuckles of the forefinger and middle finger.

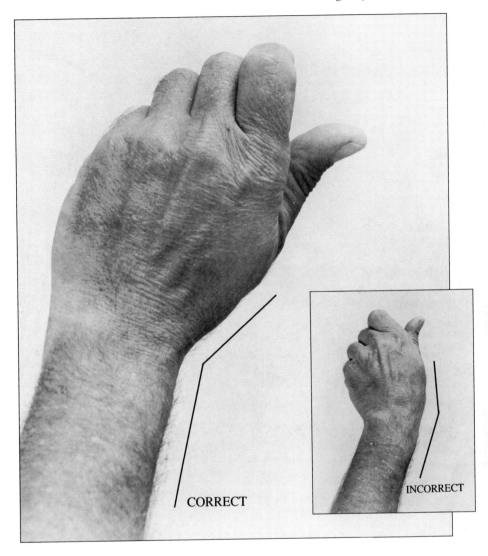

CORRECT

INCORRECT

Now bend your wrist. Bring your thumb toward your nose.

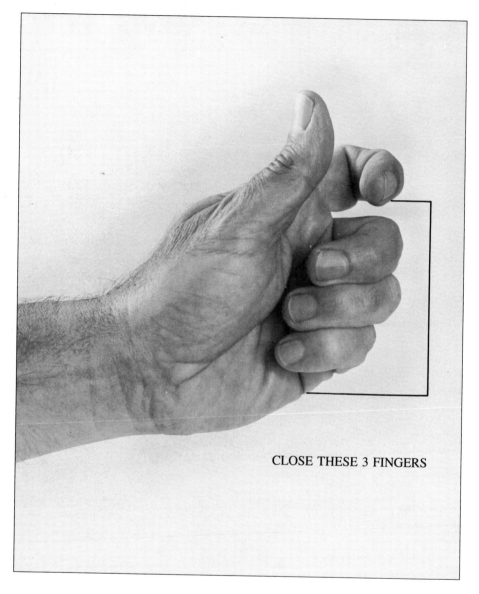

CLOSE THESE 3 FINGERS

Close the left hand as though you were squeezing a small lemon with the last three fingers (not the thumb and forefinger) against the inside of the palm.

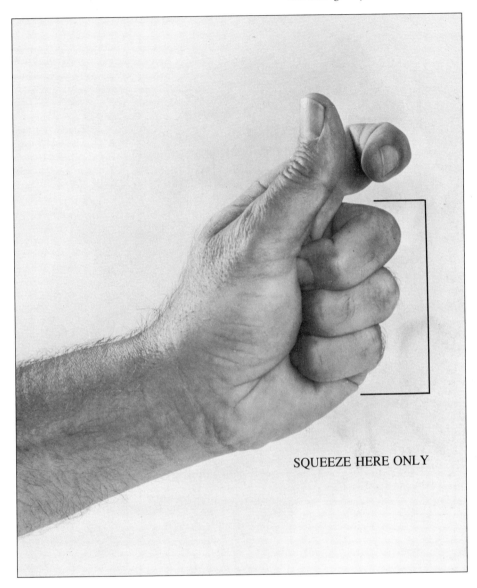

SQUEEZE HERE ONLY

Open and close to make sure the squeezing action is being induced by the last three fingers and that your wrist has maintained its upward bend (thumb toward nose). Maintain that "pose" with your left hand.

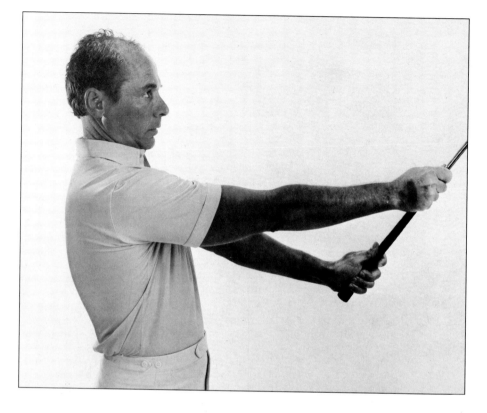

Your right hand is still holding the club and your left hand is "posed." Now place your left hand on top of the club handle as shown. The left thumb is "short" and the left forefinger "long." This encourages placing the club under control of the last three fingers and palm. The visual check for rotational placement is seeing the two top knuckles of the left forefinger and middle finger.

Place your left hand on the club by bringing it over and down on the grip with both arms straight. As shown, the club is extended well out from your body.

Do not change the angle of the club.

Grip the club with the last three fingers of the left hand, providing the total support.

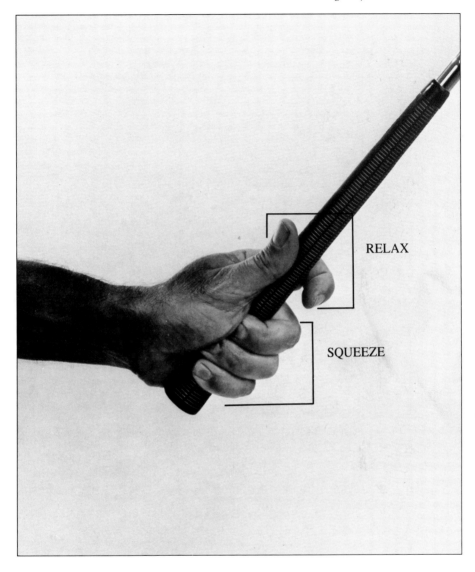

Relax the thumb and forefinger of the left hand to make certain you are gripping with the last three fingers.

If the club flops when you relax the thumb and forefinger, start all over again. Don't try to fix a mistake in the middle of the procedure.

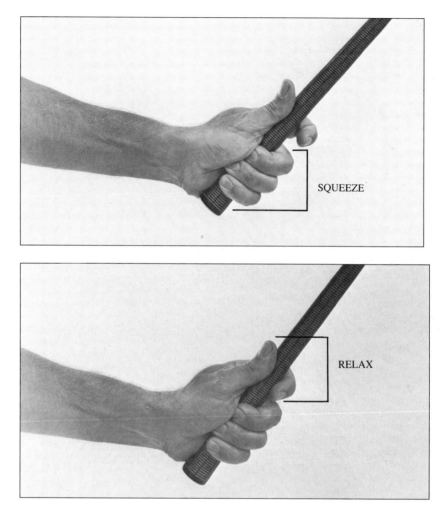

LEFT-HAND CHECKPOINTS

1) Squeeze firmly with the last three fingers.

2) Thumb lying flat and relaxed against upper portion of forefinger.

3) Wrist bent at 45° angle.

4) Pocket between ligaments just to the right of center of club.

5) Two knuckles visible.

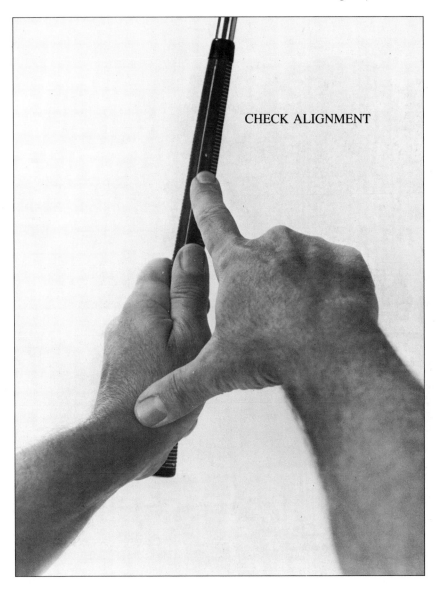

CHECK ALIGNMENT

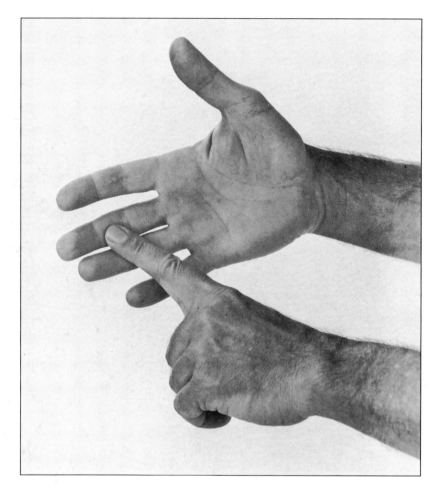

RIGHT HAND

The right hand holds the club with the first and third pads of the middle and ring fingers, the areas shown here. There should be no other pressure felt, except in the crook of the forefinger. This forefinger pressure is a residual pressure created by the proper placement and squeezing with the middle two fingers.

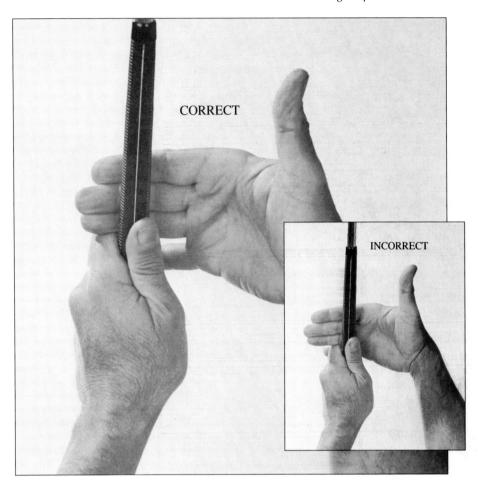

The club must not be allowed to roll into the crease between the third pad and palm. And there must be no pressure of the right thumb on the shaft. The function of the right hand is only to stabilize the club through impact.

Here's how:

Locate the middle two pads of the middle and ring fingers.

Place the middle two pads of these fingers directly under the club and touching your left hand, as shown.

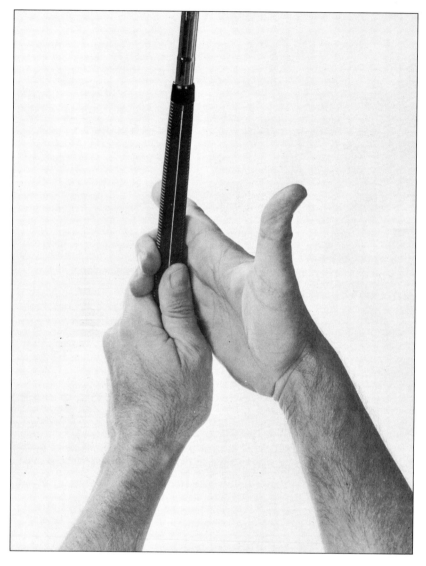

Close the middle and ring fingers of your right hand on the club.

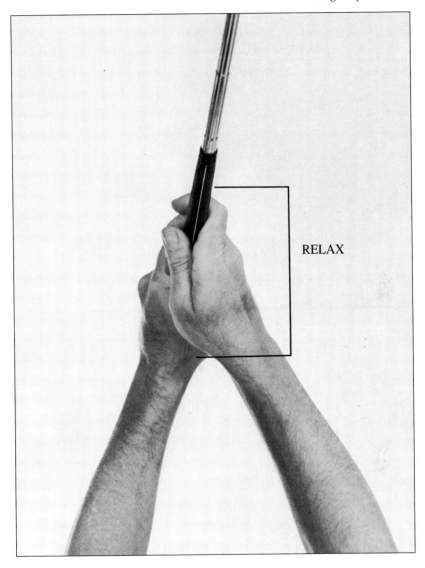

RELAX

Relax the right hand down on the left. Do not squeeze the left hand.

The pressure in the right-hand grip should only be on the middle and ring fingers around the club, with slight residual pressure in the crook of the forefinger.

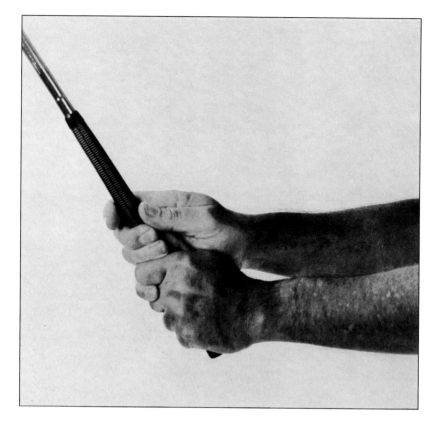

TOTAL GRIP CHECKPOINTS

1) Main pressure is in the last three fingers of left hand.
2) Left thumb and forefinger are relaxed.
3) Right little finger overlaps the left forefinger.
4) Right-hand gripping action is light.
5) Right forefinger and thumb are relaxed.
6) Right thumb is on left side of shaft. No pressure.

That's all there is to it. It's much easier and faster to do than it is to describe. Even so, you should practice until it becomes quick, easy *and* automatic.

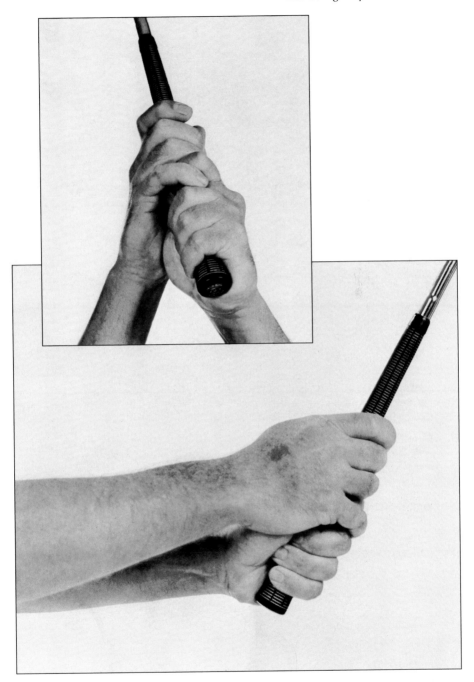

INCORRECT

GETTING INTO POSITION

Now that you've mastered the proper grip, it's time to find the right relationship between your body and the ball. While gripping the club with both hands as discussed, you've already established an approximate 45° angle between your arms and the club.

CORRECT

Now, lower the club from the shoulders, not the waist. Then as a second step simply "sit down" with your weight on the heels of your feet.

Hold the club off contact, not touching either the ball or the ground. Keep your head up in line with your spine.

CORRECT

KNEES FLEXED

CORRECT ANGLE

CLUBHEAD OFF THE GROUND

Now point your chin slightly to the right. Left foot is turned slightly out.

You have now achieved the proper standing position. Practice all of the previous steps repeatedly before proceeding.

1) Establish the correct angle between the club and arms.

2) Flex your knees and "sit down." Keep the clubhead off the ground. Point your chin slightly to the right. Turn out your left foot a bit.

THREE
THE GOLF MOTOR MOVE

Now you are going to produce the proper swing motion through the application of what I call the *Golf Motor Move*.

When you first start applying the golf motor move, it is likely that you will find your left hand not yet strong enough to support the club throughout the move without flopping.

Your strength, rhythm, balance, flexibility and coordination will improve rapidly if you practice the motor move every day without a ball.

FRONT VIEW: CORRECT POSITION BEFORE STARTER MOVE

MOVE STARTS HERE

THE MOTOR MOVE STARTER

The golf motor has a starter. The starter move is initiated by the right foot and knee (for right-handers; opposite for lefties), with the first motion in the direction of the target.

SIDE VIEW: CORRECT POSITION BEFORE
STARTER MOVE

MOVE STARTS
HERE

THE MOTOR MOVE EXERCISE

To experience and enhance your golf motor, and therefore your golf swing, master this exercise as shown in the following eight photos:

1) Grip the club in the *left hand only.*

2) Start the motion with the right foot and knee, pushing slightly to the left.

3-4) Then allow the left foot and knee to "pendulum" the action back to the right.

5-7) Follow through with a "sitting down" motion. Don't use your hands, arms or shoulders to power the club.

8) Don't stop after one swing. Respond immediately into a backswing from the finish position of the through swing.

As you practice this exercise, you will automatically begin to feel and distinctly learn the correct golf swing motion. This motion is an acquired knack that, once learned, is never lost.

This exercise is the correct way to develop your swing. You won't do it by thinking, analyzing, posing or structuring.

For example, an expert cracking a whip has no concern for the relative positions of the whip throughout the motion. Any attempt to "place" the whip in various positions as part of the whole motion would only destroy the motion itself. So it is in golf.

Do this exercise until you can produce a minimum of 15 continuous, foot-and-leg-initiated swings. Doing the exercise not only develops your golf motor, but also builds your ability to produce it even more dynamically, while at the same time increasing the ability of your left hand to support the club throughout this powerful move.

Therefore, this exercise should, for a time, replace all other practice or play. Only after you can produce a minimum of 15 dynamic, left-hand-only swings should you add your right hand.

4

3

5

6

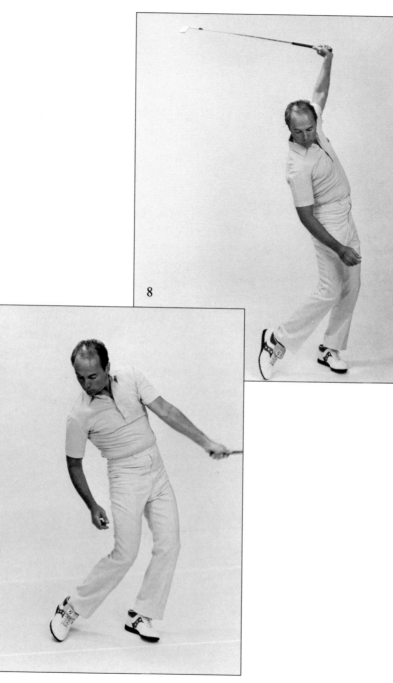

CHECK YOUR MOTOR MOVE EXERCISE

After you can produce a continuous back-and-forth swing using just your legs and feet, you may begin to add some extra power to the downswing. The proper way to start the downswing is best described as "sit down." The club's response to this move is the essence of the swing.

There are only two things you have to keep in mind while doing the motor move:

1) Keep your chin pointed behind the ball.

2) Initiate the downswing with a slight "sitting down" motion.

The tendency is to start the downswing with the hands or shoulders. This destroys the dynamic action of the swing.

You must start the downswing with the lower body. Just "sit down."

THE SOUND OF A CORRECT GOLF SWING

When you are producing the correct swing, you will hear a sound as the shaft moves through the air. If your wrist flops, the sound will disappear. If you initiate the downswing with your shoulders, you will hear very little sound.

EXERCISE PROGRESSION:
ADDING YOUR RIGHT HAND

As soon as you can produce 15 consecutive motor move swings while maintaining control of the club without your left wrist flopping, you are ready to add your right hand. For most players, this will require 5 to 10 days of practice. If the quality of the swing breaks down, rest a day. You'll come back stronger than ever.

Do not play golf or hit any ball during this period.

Now with the right hand on as shown earlier, repeat the motor move exercise. Practice this until the motion, the sound and the feel are the same with either the left hand only or both hands on the club.

The right hand, though adding dramatically to the shot by stabilizing the club through impact, adds nothing to the swing itself. Any voluntary or involuntary introduction of right-hand "action" is an attempt to either control the backswing or speed up the through-swing. Both are counter-productive.

For this reason, you must, *must, MUST* place the right hand on the club as previously described, with the club held lightly in the middle of the middle and ring fingers and the rest of the hand relaxed.

As you become better and better at the golf motor move, all of the positions and features you have been striving for during your golf career will simply occur as effects. The pleasurable, dynamic action of the swing itself will automatically take over, and you will be ready to hit some balls.

FOUR
Hitting The Ball

B y now you should have power in your Golf Motor Move and strength in your left hand through the exercise of the previous chapter. You can start your transition to shot-production at the practice tee with a 6, 7 or 8 iron with the ball on a tee. Eventually progress to using woods, starting with the shortest.

Use the pre-swing preparation steps of Chapter 2. Be certain to keep the clubhead out of contact with the ground or the ball. Start the motor and simply repeat the two-handed exercise through the ball.

USING AN IRON

1) Club and arms maintain the same relationship at the top of the swing as at the beginning. This is made possible by proper setup prior to the shot.

2) Wrist cock occurs (naturally) on the downswing as the leg and torso muscles pull the club back toward the ball.

3) Lower body leads swing, and shoulders begin to bring head around long after contact.

4) A high finish is the natural consequence of the proper swing.

USING A WOOD

1) Wide arc occurs naturally as a result of proper setup and initiation of the move with the lower body.

2) Position at top is the same with a driver as with short irons.

3) Chin is still pointed to the right as the swing enters the impact zone.

4) Lower body leads the swing.

BALL POSITIONING

For all clubs, the clubhead is in the same position relative to the left foot. It only appears to be different because you move the right foot to widen your stance as the club gets longer.

Position of the right foot for wedge shot.

Position of the right foot for short iron.

Position of the right foot for medium iron.

Position of the right foot for wood shot.

PROGRESSING STEP-BY-STEP

Four factors tend to inhibit anybody's golf swing:
1) The ball.
2) The target.
3) Observation by others.
4) Competition.

The longer you keep the pressure off at each level of progression, the more competent you will be at producing an uninhibited swing at the next level.

Beginning Motor Move Exercise—Swing repeatedly with left hand only. Right hand off club. Make the sound of a correct golf swing. See page 53.

Intermediate Motor Move Exercise—Both hands on the club. Hit balls, still using an iron. Make the sound of a correct golf swing.

Advanced Motor Move Exercise—Same as intermediate level, but use longer clubs. Graduate to your longest wood.

DOING IT WRONG

Compare the following incorrect sequence with the previous correct sequences. Notice how unhappy I look demonstrating an incorrect swing.

1) Loose, floppy wrists and locked knees. Notice the absence of retained energy in the shaft.

2) Again, we see locked knees and a wristy swing instead of dynamic body involvement in the impact area.

3) With this type of "swing," there is no solid contact or high finish.

BACK VIEW

DOING IT RIGHT

Compact position at the top of the swing is the automatic result of the proper setup and lower body involvement in the backswing.

1) Here I am in a perfect plane without having to think about it. The club is completely under control because of the proper grip.

BACK VIEW

2) Notice how my chin is still pointed to the right long after the ball has been "airmailed." The lower body leads the swing and pulls the club to great extension, creating on-target results.

3) With the chin back and the lower body flexed and moving, the extension through the shot happens naturally, and the club face stays right on track without manipulation.

BACK VIEW

4) A high, well-balanced finish occurs naturally when you use the Automatic Golf method.

I'll take a million shots like this. Everything is happening automatically and my only thought is keeping my chin back. The dominance of the proper swinging muscles has occurred because of the proper setup before the swing began.

FIVE
Sand Play And Other Shots

As stated earlier, the motion of an Automatic Golf swing is the same for all clubs except the putter. But not all golf shots are off of a tee, which means you often have to contend with other variables. In this chapter I address a variety of these variables and offer some elegant solutions to some difficult situations.

HIGH LIE

If the ball is sitting up, as shown above, the objective is to pass the club *under* the ball by using the golf motor move.

To do this, open the face of the club by turning its toe to the right before gripping. This reduces the height of the club and allows it to pass more easily under the ball.

This is a good lie, but a bunker lip looms.

To make the shot, move a lot of sand to get the ball up quickly over the lip.

BALL IN DEPRESSION OR SLIGHTLY BURIED

In this situation, you should open the club blade more than normal to allow easy passage of the blade under the ball.

A flatter blade angle moves minimal sand.

BURIED LIE

If the ball is more than slightly buried, you cannot extract it by passing the blade under it. Any attempt to do so will likely produce a skulled, fast-moving shot that lands in never-never land. This happens because the blade can't pass under the ball and so strikes it directly. The solution is to close the blade as shown.

The action allows the toe of the club to enter the sand first, which will pop the ball out of the buried lie.

Warning: This shot will come out very "hot," so apply very little force. Hope that you have a lot of green to work with.

MISCELLANEOUS SAND MUSINGS

Be sure to apply these principles with all sand shots:
The leg action is the same as it is on full shots.

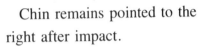

Chin remains pointed to the right after impact.

As with other types of shots, good extension is the product of proper action.

HITTING THE BALL LOW

To lower the trajectory of any fairway shot, simply position the ball closer toward the right foot. Nothing else needs to change.
Here is the normal position for normal straight shots.

Use this ball position for hitting the ball lower with the same club.

HITTING A HIGH SHOT

To raise the trajectory of any fairway shot, simply position the ball forward toward the left foot. Again, nothing else changes.

FADING THE BALL LEFT TO RIGHT

To fade this shot I have withdrawn my left foot back from the line of flight and opened the blade slightly. This changes the angle of attack.

DRAWING THE BALL RIGHT TO LEFT

Close the stance (opposite of open). Note: Neither fading nor drawing should be attempted by manipulating the club during the swing. The action remains the same; only the angle of attack changes, as shown.

When your right foot is withdrawn, the line of flight changes the angle of attack at contact. This imparts the desired right-to-left flight.

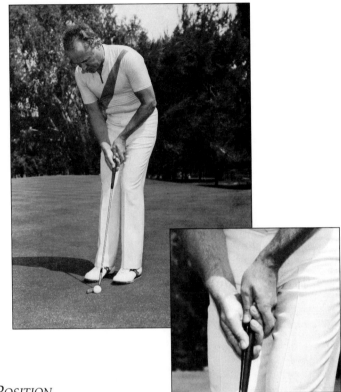

Putting Position

Good putters apply a minimum amount of force to make the ball move a given distance. To accomplish this, it's necessary to maintain loft on the putter throughout the stroke. This prevents pinching the ball into the green. Pinching typically occurs when golfers manipulate the club with wrist cock during the back stroke.

As you look at my starting position, you will see that I have maintained the loft on the putter by keeping my hands back to the right, in line with the putter head.

I use the *reverse overlap* grip—all of the fingers of the right hand on the shaft. This is merely the style I have adopted and is not mandatory. You can use any grip that you prefer for putting. (Remember: The Automatic Golf grip described earlier in this book *is mandatory* to produce reliable results with all other clubs.)

My weight is equally balanced on both feet. Many (right-handed) golfers concentrate their weight on the left leg while putting. Doing this reduces putter loft, something you don't want. Maintaining putter loft is the key element in a good stroke. Stay equally balanced.

PUTTING STROKE

An efficient putting stroke is the picture of simplicity.

1) The starting position of the hands is maintained as you simply move the club back without wrist cock or any other extraneous motion.

2) The follow-through is the mirror image of unmanipulated simplicity.

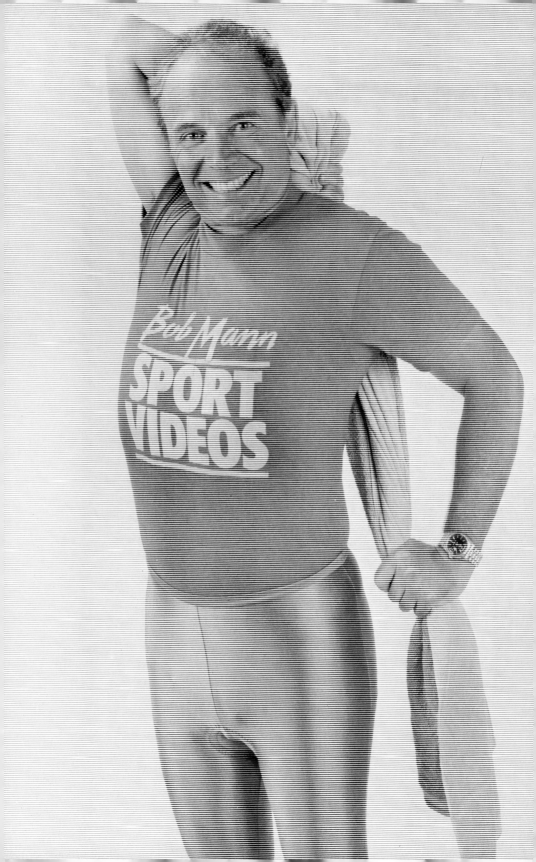

SIX
FITNESS FOR GOLFERS

You don't have to be a strongwoman or strongman to be a good golfer. True power comes from the dynamic action created by the muscles in your legs and torso. Even so, physical fitness does contribute to a better game.

You'll find the exercises of this chapter beneficial if you do them two or more times per week. A good routine will require only a few minutes per exercise, yet will pay substantial dividends in your golf game and overall well-being.

There is no magic number of repetitions. Start with whatever number is comfortable for you. But be sure to keep track of your progress. This way, you can increase the number of reps as your fitness improves.

HAND AND WRIST
STRENGTH TO
SUPPORT CLUB

FLEXIBILITY PERMITS
FULL TURN WITHOUT
STRAIN

LEG AND TORSO
MUSCLES POWER
CLUB

The physical attributes required to produce an effective swing are:

√ Hand and wrist strength to support (not propel) the club.

√ Leg and torso strength for power throughout the golf motor move.

√ Overall flexibility for smooth, coordinated body motion.

SHOULDER FLEXIBILITY

Grasp a towel as shown and pull down with lower hand. Apply a steady pull, not a snap or jerking action. Keep elbow of upper arm close to your ear. Hold for approximately 30 seconds.

Repeat on other side.

WRIST AND HAND EXERCISE

Wring a dry or wet towel until you feel the muscles in your forearms tighten. Then wring it out a bit more.

SKATER'S MOVE

Do this for hip flexibility and leg strength. With your weight mostly on your heels, lower your left elbow to the inside of your left knee while bending your left leg.

Remain low and bend your right leg. Lower your right elbow to the inside of your right knee. The movement of this marvelous exercise is swiveling from side to side.

Minimize up and down movement as you switch from right to left. By keeping your weight on your heels and moving from side to side, you will firm your backside while increasing your leg strength and hip mobility.

LUNGE

Step forward and lower your body while keeping your upper body erect. Alternate legs for as many repetitions as comfortable.

The lunge is another leg strengthener, backside firmer and hip-flexibility enhancer.

Mini-Plié

Stand erect with your toes pointed well out to the sides. Lower while holding your upper body erect. You have to lower only a few inches to receive benefits for your legs. This is another great backside firmer *if* you concentrate on keeping your upper body erect and fanny tightened while doing this exercise.

You will be comfortable doing many more repetitions of this exercise than either the skater's move or lunge.

WALL SIT

This one looks easy, and it is for a short time. But the benefits come in the form of rapid increase in leg strength if you hold the position longer than is comfortable.

Sit against a wall without a seat under you for as long as comfortable and then for 10, 20 or 30 seconds more.

MOTOR MOVE EXERCISE

Even after you have graduated to the golf course, make the motor move exercise part of your exercise routine. Strive to achieve 15, or more, proper swings in a row.

SEVEN
SUMMING UP

When you need a quick refresher on various aspects of the Automatic Golf method, refer to this handy photographic summary. If it doesn't refresh your memory, refer to the more detailed analyses in earlier chapters.

As with any important skill, improving your golf game requires practice and dedication. There are no instant, overnight solutions. But the Automatic Golf method does make mastering this enjoyable game as simple as possible. More than 400,000 satisfied owners of the *Automatic Golf* video agree with me. I hope you do too. Good luck.

With proper setup before the shot, the swing becomes virtually automatic. The proper setup includes the grip, achieved step-by-step as described in Chapter 2.

The relationship of club to arms is not changed as you lower into the starting position, or throughout the swing.

Knees flexed; weight on heels; head up; chin to the right; left foot turned slightly toward target. Club off contact with ground or ball.

Motion begins with lower body press toward target.

Backswing is initiated by the legs, as response-action to the forward press.

"Sit down" to begin downswing, keep chin pointed to right.

SAND SHOTS

The main objective of sand shots is to pass the club under ball using the motor move. (The exception is a buried lie. See page 88).

Hit high, low, fade or draw shots by changing position. Use the same swinging action.

PROGRESSION TO BETTER GOLF AUTOMATICALLY

1) Grip.
2) Starting position.
3) Golf motor move without ball; left hand only.
4) Motor move with both hands.
5) Hit balls at practice range without observers, with a tee, using a 6, 7 or 8 iron.
6) Progress to longer clubs, as in #5.
7) Remove tee at practice range.
8) Play alone with tee.
9) Play alone without tee, except for tee shots.
10) Play in a group.
11) Compete.

Index

A
advanced golfer, 9
average golfer, 9

B
balance, 45
ball position, 68-71
beginning golfer, 9
buried lie, 86, 88

C
centrifugal force, 15
chin, 42, 78, 91
clubhead speed, 16
cocking, 15, 18
coordination, 45

D
David, 15
delayed hit, 15
downswing, 18
drawing, 96
dynamic motion, 13

E
energy, shaft, 17
exercises, 101-109

F
fading, 95
finish, 63
flexibility, 45, 102

G
Goliath, 15
grip, 21-37
grooved swing, 14

H
hand exercise, 104
high finish, 15, 63
high lie, 84
high shot, 94
hub, 16

I
iron shots, 60-63

J
jade parable, 13

L
left-hand grip, 24-27
low shot, 92
lunge, 106

The **Automatic Golf** video is available in local bookstores and wherever fine videos are sold. Or, order it by mail by sending $14.95, plus $2.00 postage and handling to Video Reel, 28231 N. Ave. Crocker, Suite 120, Valencia, CA 91355. Specify VHS or Beta.

Other Bob Mann Sports Videos available:
Isometric Stretch & **Instant Karate**

Thank you for making the **Automatic Golf** video the #1 selling sports video worldwide.

Bob Mann

—